Sports Stars

MARY DECKER

America's Nike

By Cathy Henkel

 CHILDRENS PRESS, CHICAGO

Cover photograph: Charlie Nye
Inside photographs courtesy of the following:
Charlie Nye, pages 6, 9, 13, 15, 17, 22, 28, 31, 33, 35, 37, and 39
Victor G. Sailer, pages 11, 20, 24, 26, and 41

Library of Congress Cataloging in Publication Data

Henkel, Cathy.
  Mary Decker, America's Nike.

  (Sports stars)
  Summary: A brief biography of the woman considered to
be the fastest runner in the world.
    1. Decker, Mary, 1958-   —Juvenile literature.
2. Runners (Sports)—United States—Biography—Juvenile
literature. [1. Decker, Mary, 1958-   . 2. Runners (Sports)]
I. Title. II. Series.
GV1061.15.D42H46   1984   796.4'26 [B] [92] 83-25265
ISBN 0-516-04338-2

1 2 3 4 5 6 7 8 9 10 R 93 92 91 90 89 88 87 86 85 84

Sports Stars

MARY DECKER

America's Nike

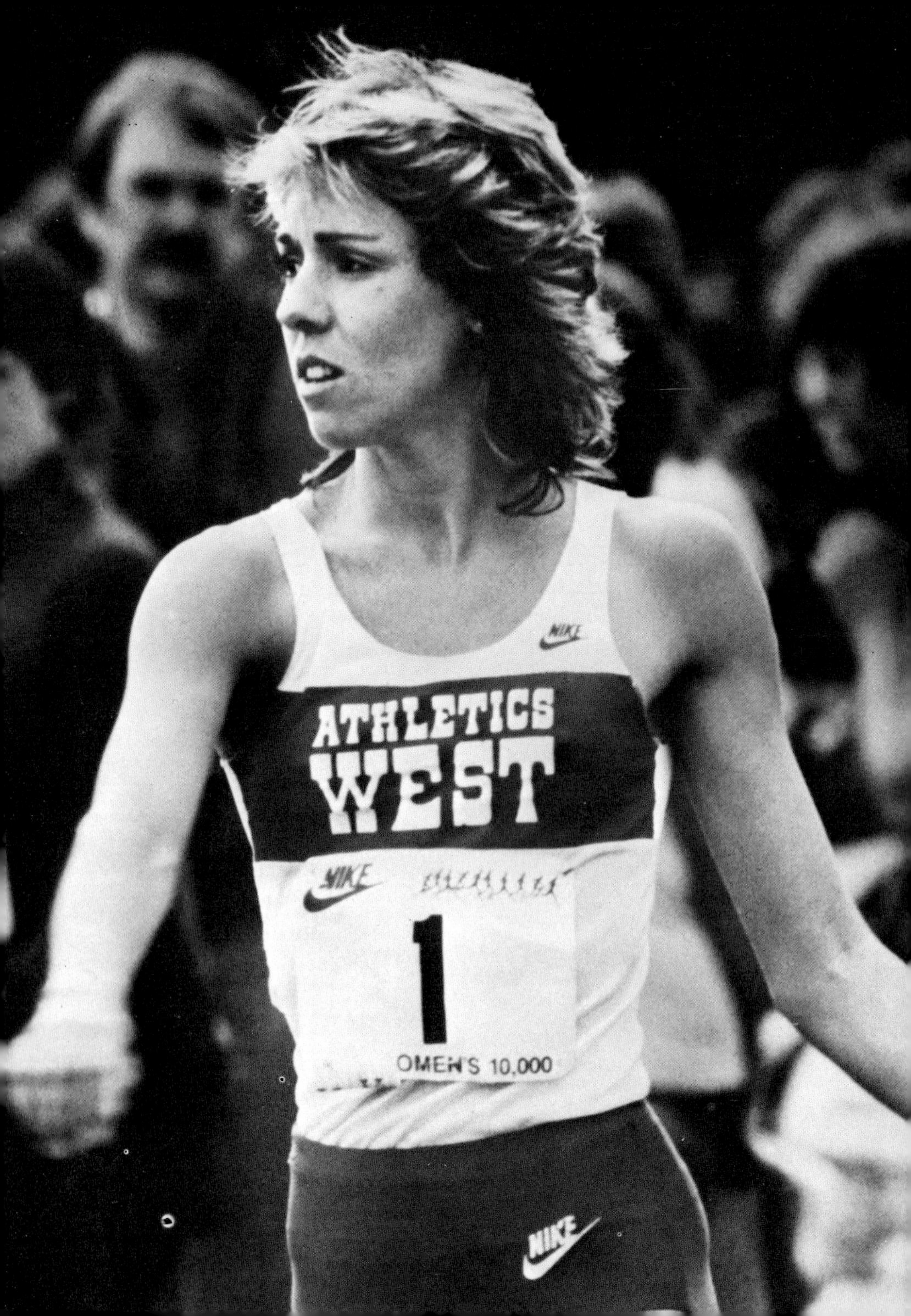
NIKE
ATHLETICS
WEST
NIKE
1
OMEN'S 10,000
NIKE

She was 15 and a long way from home. Mary Decker was just a teenager then. It was her birthday. But she was not eating ice cream and cake with her family in California. She was eating spaghetti in a hotel in Senegal, a faraway land on the northwest tip of Africa. She was there with the best runners from her country. Tomorrow, they would run against the best runners from Africa.

Suddenly, it was quiet. A line of tall, black men in white robes walked into the room. They walked right up to Mary and stopped. She tried to hide in her chair. One of the men bent over and gave her some roses. Another man gave her a birthday gift. He said it was from the leader of Senegal. It was a bronze statue of an African soldier on a horse. Her teammates stood up and sang "Happy Birthday." She hugged the beautiful statue and smiled. She was so happy she cried.

The next day Mary won the race against the Africans. Ten years later, she is still winning races. And she still has the statue. It sits on a shelf in her living room. It is not alone. Many trophies are there, too. They remind her of her many victories, awards, and world records. But one thing is missing. An Olympic medal. She has run fast for 14 years. But she has never been to the Olympics.

"I won't be happy until I win a gold medal," says Mary, who is now 25 years old. "It's something I've always wanted to do. When my running is finished, I want to look back and say I did it. I put all I had into the sport."

Mary is one of the world's fastest runners. But she is unlucky, it seems. When it was time for the 1972 Olympics, Mary was one of the best in the half mile. But she was only 14. They said she was too young to compete in the Olympics. So she had to stay home when the U.S. Olympic team went to Munich.

When it was time for the 1976 Olympics, Mary was old enough. She was 18. But every time she ran, it hurt. She went to see many doctors. They told her not to run. But she could not stop. She loved to run. It hurt so much, though, that she finally had to stop. But Mary did not feel sorry for herself. She moved to Boulder, Colorado. She took a job selling shoes to other runners. And she waited until she could run again.

"I just kept telling myself that my time would come," Mary said.

Mary sold shoes to runners when she could not run. She didn't feel sorry for herself.

She met a man who was also a runner. His name was Dick Quax. He asked her why she didn't run anymore. She told him that her legs hurt too much. He told her that his legs hurt once, too. He had surgery. A doctor fixed his legs. He showed her the scars on his shins. He told Mary to go to the same doctor. She did, and had surgery, too. It worked!

A month after the operation, Mary was running again. She had no pain. But it was too late. The 1976 Olympics in Montreal were over.

Mary didn't care, though, not then. She was young and still had plenty of time to run in the Olympics. Besides, she could finally run again.

Running is not all runners do. They have to stretch so their muscles work well.

"It was such a treat," she said. "I just really love to run. I never say 'I have to run today.' I say 'Hey, I get to run today.'"

And how she ran. In her first race after the operation, Mary set a world record for 1,000 yards indoors. She also won the national collegiate cross-country championships.

The next year, Mary moved to Eugene, Oregon. They call the town the Track Capital. It seems like everyone in the town runs or likes to watch other people run. Mary thought this would be a great place for her to live and train for the Olympics.

In Eugene, she found a club called Athletics West. It was a team sponsored by the Nike running shoe company. It was for the country's best runners. It was for men only, but they asked Mary to join.

"They kind of bent the rules for me," Mary laughs.

Mary is still with the team. Other women have followed her to the club. Joan Benoit, who has the world record for the women's marathon, belongs. Men still belong. Alberto Salazar, who holds the men's record for the marathon, belongs. The marathon is a very long distance—26 miles and 385 yards. Mary says she may even run one some day.

Mary goes to the club at least three times each week for a massage. She also goes there to talk to her coach, Dick Brown. He laughs when he says his main job is to hold Mary back.

"She's genetically gifted," says the coach. "God went zap and her genes came together. After that, it's a matter of not allowing her to over-train and get hurt."

Mary has been hurt more than once. "Injuries are an athlete's nightmare," she says. "After every one, I try to find a fresh approach to attack it. But it's more like cry baby one time and scream baby the next. You do some funny things. It's just not the same for me when I can't run."

Mary has had many injuries. When she was 15, she caught her foot in her bicycle spokes and cracked it. At 16, she broke her foot again. At 17, her feet were in casts for two months. At 18, she had surgery. At 19, she hurt her back. At 22, she had two more operations on her legs. At 23, she broke her ankle. At 24, she got whiplash when a milk truck rammed her car from behind.

You wonder if she runs so fast to get away from anything that might hurt her again.

"I've had everything," Mary sighs. "But the only thing I regret about those injuries is that they kept me out of the Olympics."

In 1980 Mary won first place in the 1,500 meters in the Olympic Trials in Eugene, Oregon.

Mary was not hurt when it came time for the 1980 Olympics in Moscow. In fact, she had a great year. She started off by running four world records in one month. She won the 1,500 meters in the Olympic Trials in Eugene. But this time, politics kept her home. President Carter said the Americans could not be in the Olympics because the Russian army had invaded Afganistan. Mary wanted to go very much. She was sad that she had to stay home. But there was nothing she could do.

Then, in 1983, the countries of the world got together for a track meet in Helsinki, Finland.

After winning a race in Knoxville, Tennessee in 1982, Mary watches the other runners come in.

Everyone was there. They called it the World Track and Field Championships. It was the first time besides the Olympics that all the countries had come to a track meet.

Mary had become so good in America that no one in her own country could beat her. She had won every race for four years. Since the other Americans could not keep up with her, she raced against the clock. She tried to beat the clock. She tried to run faster and faster. She was always by herself—way up front. In the World Championships that would change. She would finally get a chance to run against the powerful Russians and East Germans. No one knew if she was strong enough to run with them.

For Mary, running is fun!

When Mary got to Finland, her coach said she would enter two races. That was a shock. It is hard to run in more than one race. But Mary felt good. She wanted to try it. The first race was the 3,000 meters, a little longer than two miles. Mary took the lead at the start. She never gave it up. She beat the Russian star, Tatyana Kazankina, who had won two Olympic gold medals. She also beat another Russian who held the world record.

"I felt strong and in control," Mary said after the race. "I just took a deep breath and relaxed. I haven't had a lot of practice with my kick at home. It was fun to have competition."

Mary is serious about running. She wishes more women would compete with her.

Mary now had one medal. But there was still one more race to go. It was the 1,500 meters, the metric mile. Would she be too tired to take on the rest of the Russians?

When the race began, she took the lead again.

"I didn't know if someone else would want to lead, or if they would let me lead," she said. "If someone else wanted to lead, I would have let them. I didn't want to lead the pace into a strong wind and then find I didn't have what I needed at the end."

But no one else led, so Mary did. She led all the way until the last turn. One of the Russian runners, Zamira Zaitseva, bolted around her.

"She leaned into me and I had to back off," said Mary.

But Mary would not give up. She had been through too much. She picked up the pace and ran like crazy. She gritted her teeth as she pulled up beside Zaitseva. The finish line was just a few yards ahead. Zaitseva dove for the finish, but fell. She rolled past the finish line, but she was beaten. Mary stayed on her feet and sprinted past.

Mary had won two medals. She had beaten the Russians. She had beaten the best in the world.

Mary's fans love to watch her run and win, and they also like to have her autograph.

"This is the closest I've come to the Olympic Games," Mary said. "People who know my history know what this means to me."

The Russian runners did not know what to say.

"I think we will change our tactics and find something new," said Zaitseva. "Mary has prepared very well this year. It is difficult to say what we will do."

Mary knows exactly what she must do. She must stay healthy if she wants to go to her first Olympics. She will be 26 when it's time for the Olympics in Los Angeles. She will be very careful and train very hard. She will run 6 to 10

miles each day, but never more than 60 miles a week. She will listen to her coach.

"I will probably try even harder in Los Angeles. Everyone will be very excited," said Mary. "But I can't give away any secrets. I will try to find a quiet place and get away from all the distractions. I need to concentrate."

Mary will still go to the Athletics West club in Eugene. She will get her massages. Rich Phaigh rubs her famous calves very hard to make them feel better.

"Below the knees, Mary's legs are a mass of scar tissue and knots," explains Rich Phaigh. "She had tendinitis sometimes, shin splints, and muscle tears, all of which create new scar tissue.

Mary has had all kinds of trouble with her legs, but she still runs.

I have to work harder on Mary's calves than on anyone else's."

But Mary takes it in stride. She will not use drugs. She gets very mad when people say she might be taking steroids. Steroids are drugs that can make women as strong and muscular as men. Sometimes, steroids make women look like men. Mary does not look like that. She is thin and pretty. She paints her fingernails. She even wears lipstick and earrings when she races.

"I like being feminine," she says. "And that's how it is. It makes me feel good that I can do something the Eastern European runners have done without doing the things they've had to do, like taking steroids."

Mary likes to look nice. She wears makeup and jewelry. She does not take steroids.

So how can Mary be so good? How can she be so much better than everyone else?

"That is the hardest question for me to answer," Mary says. "I'm asked that all the time. I really don't know the answer. I can't believe it's because I train harder. I can't believe it's because I'm the only person in this country physically capable. I wish I knew the answer and I think a few more people wish they knew, too."

"The track is Mary's stage," said one coach. "She's just like a movie star."

Mary laughs. "I do have a touch of ham in me," she says.

Mary's coach says the track is her stage.

The spotlight focused on her at a young age. She started running when she was 11. She was bored and had nothing else to do. She and a friend read a flyer about a cross-country race. They entered. Mary's friend quit, but Mary didn't. In fact, she won, and by "a whole lot."

Mary wants to continue to win. She wants an Olympic medal. A gold one.

"This time, nothing will stop me," she says. "I've had so many goals in my head for so long. When I was injured I couldn't say anything. All you can do is wait to get well and hope that things will be right some day so you can do what you really want to do. Now these things

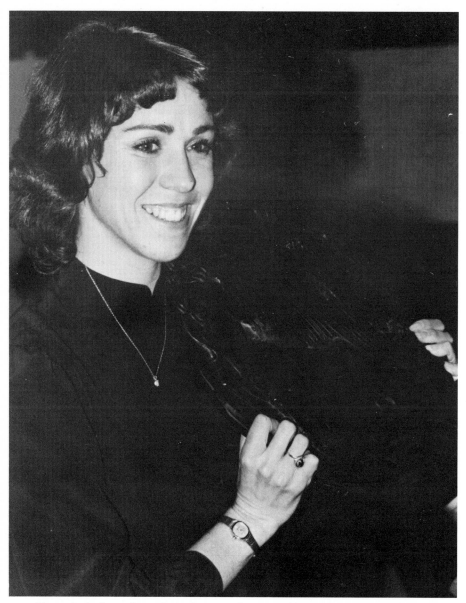

Mary started running when she was eleven and has won many medals and awards.

are happening to me. If it's a dream, I don't want to wake up."

What would happen if Mary did get injured again? Could she stand it?

"Each time I've been hurt, it's just made me more determined to come back again. I could be injured tomorrow and have to take another year off. But I can tell you right now, I'd be back."

CHRONOLOGY

1958—Mary Teresa Decker is born in Bunnvale, New Jersey, on August 4.

1968—Mary moves with her family to Santa Ana, California, then to Huntington Beach, California.

1969—Mary runs her first race and wins.

1970—Mary runs in her first and only marathon. She is timed in three hours and nine minutes.

1971—Mary sets her first record, in the half mile, a national record for her age group, 13. She wins the Mt. SAC Relays.

1972—At 14, Mary is ranked as one of the best in the half mile but cannot compete in the Olympics becuase she is too young.

1973—Mary captures three indoor world records. She travels to Europe and Africa with the American team.

1974—Mary sets the indoor world record for the half mile, and then beats the Russians in the U.S.-U.S.S.R. track meet.

1975—Mary begins to have pains in her shins and it is hard to run.

1976—By now, Mary is nearly crippled by shin pain and can't run at all. She graduates from high school and moves to Boulder, Colorado. Again, the Olympics go on without her.

1977—Mary enrolls at the University of Colorado and tries to run again. She soon is diagnosed with stress fractures and is put in a cast for nearly three months. It doesn't help so she has a special operation. She is finally running again, without pain.

1978—Mary begins setting records again. In her first major U.S. race in three years, she sets the indoor 1,000-yard world record. She also wins the national collegiate cross-country meet. She suffers from a sciatic nerve problem and has more surgery.

1979—Mary runs an American record in the mile. She wins a gold medal in the Pan Am Games in the 1,500 meters. She loses for the last time to an American, at the national championships. She moves to Eugene, Oregon and joins Athletics West.

1980—Mary sets four world records in four weeks: the outdoor mile, the indoor mile, the 1,500, and the 880. She wins the 1,500 in the U.S. Olympic Trials, but misses the Olympics because of the American boycott.

1981—Mary is hurt, has surgery twice, and misses the entire season.

1982—Mary sets the world record in the mile in Paris, an American record in the 3,000 meters in Oslo, a world record in the 5,000 meters in Eugene, and a world record in the 10,000 in Eugene. She is the only woman to earn a world ranking in five events: 800, 1,500, 3,000, 5,000, and 10,000. She is named the top amateur athlete in the United States.

1983—Mary wins two gold medals in the World Track and Field Championships in Helsinki, Finland, in the 1,500 and 3,000. She sets her goals for the 1984 Olympics in Los Angeles.

ABOUT THE AUTHOR

Cathy Henkel has worked for newspapers for 16 years, starting in her hometown of Wichita, Kansas. She currently is a sports writer for *The Register-Guard* in Eugene, Oregon. In Eugene, she watched Mary run world records and talked to her when Mary could not run at all.

In Eugene, Ms. Henkel writes about track and field, college basketball, international gymnastics, and many other sports. In a way, she has followed her father's footsteps. He coached nearly every sport at a high school in Wichita. She decided to write about sports.

In 1984, Ms. Henkel will follow Mary Decker's trail to the Olympic Games in Los Angeles to see if Mary wins the gold medal.